SHETLAND PONY

COLORING BOOK

CRYSTAL
COLORING BOOKS

ISBN: 9781726778220

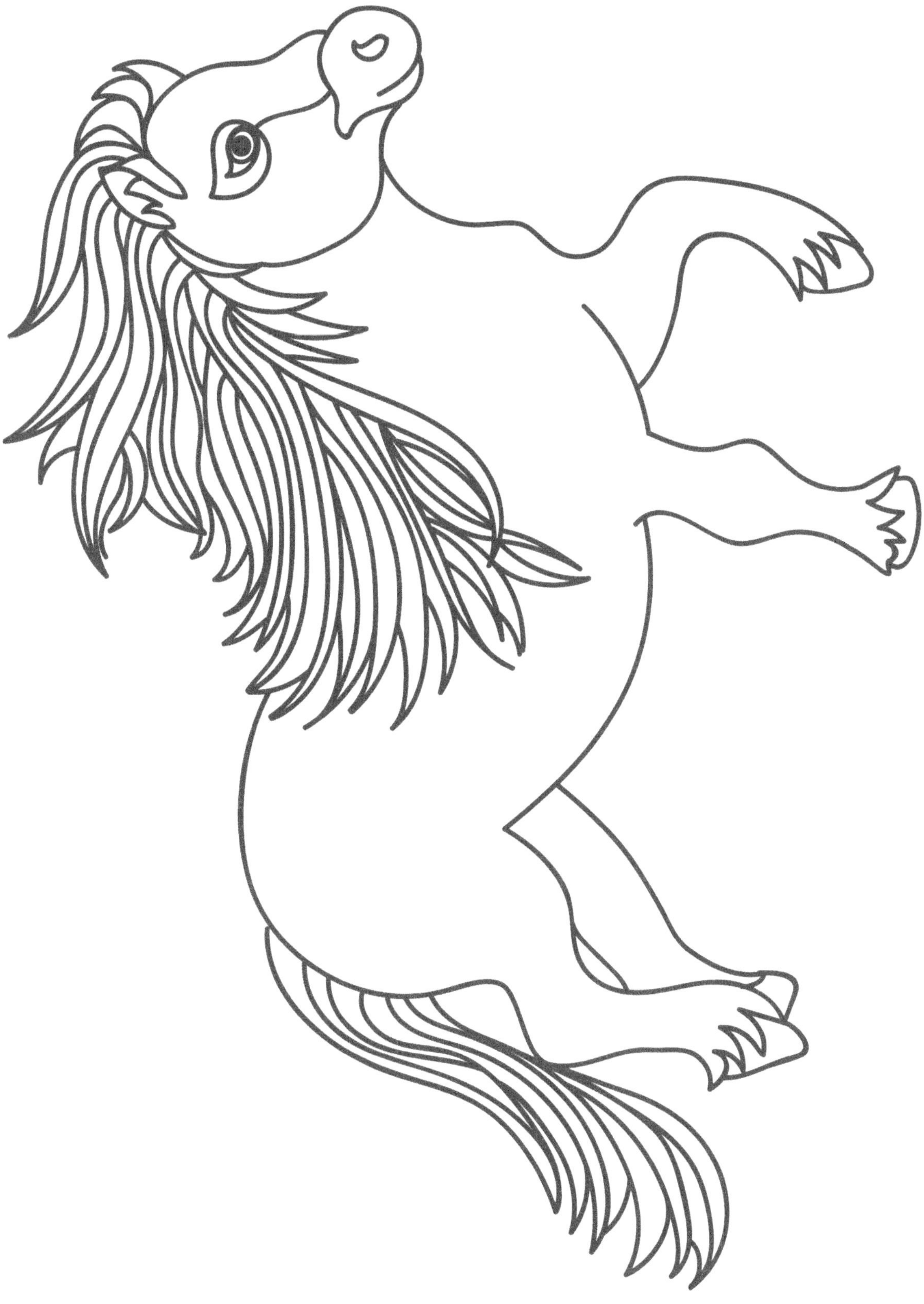

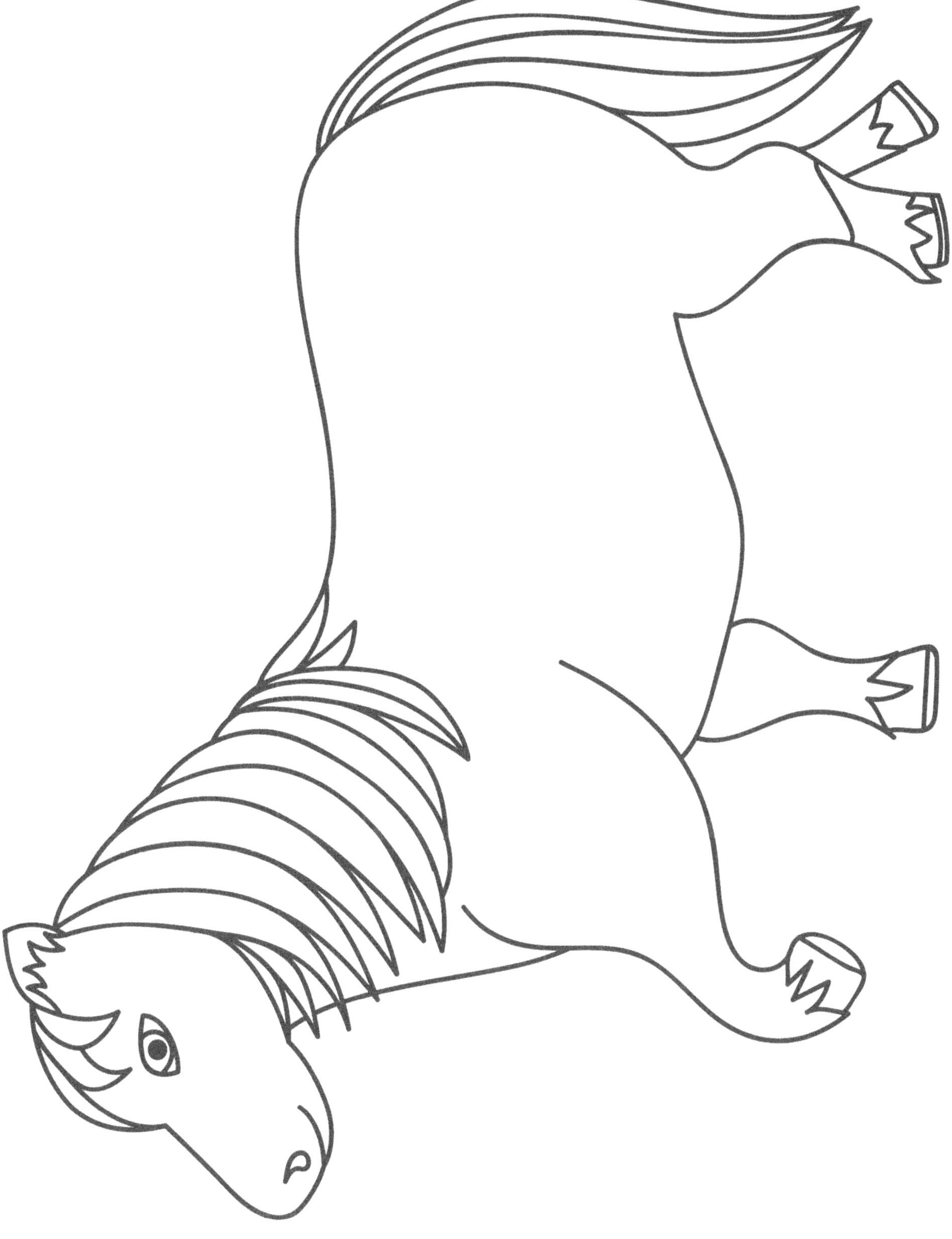

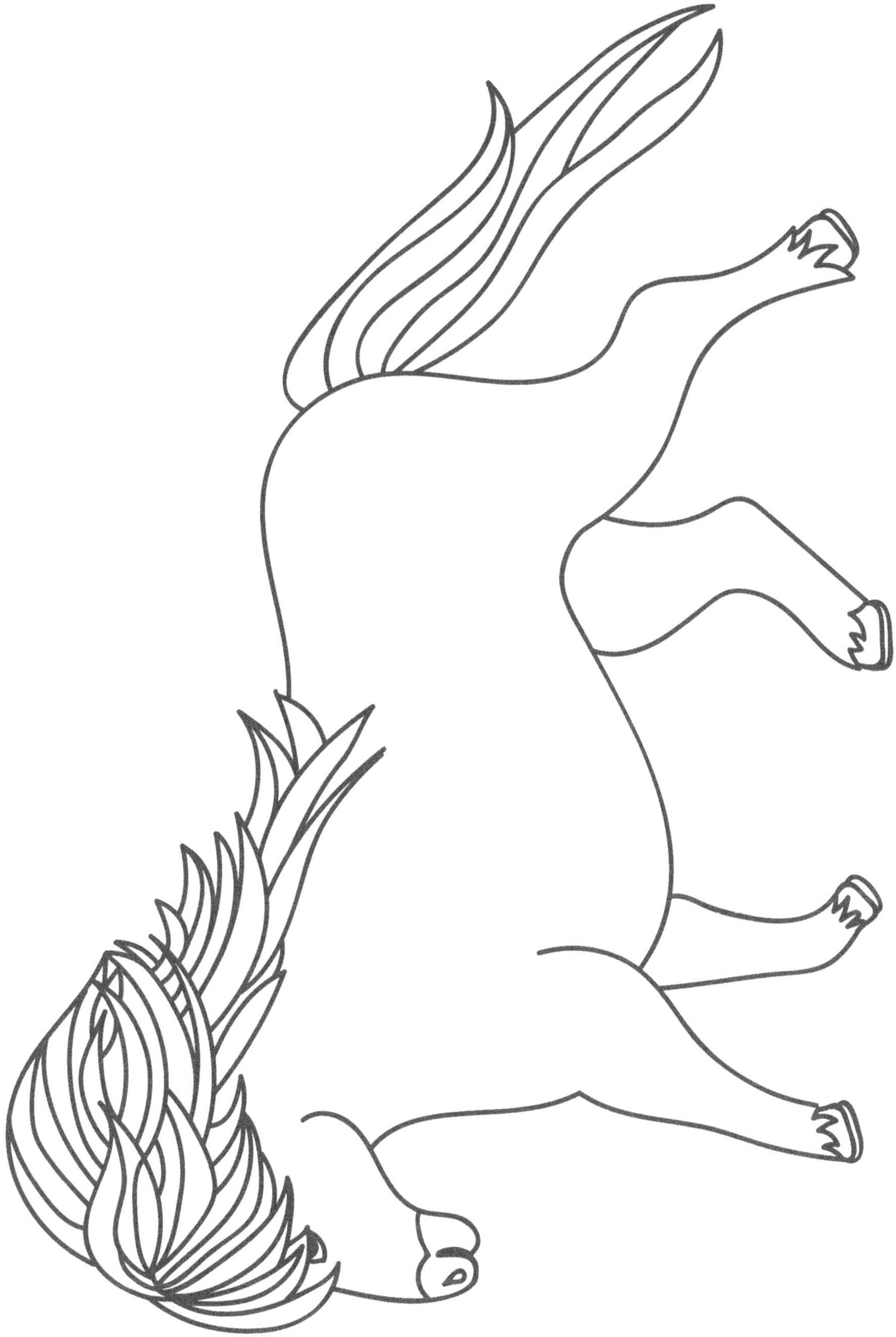

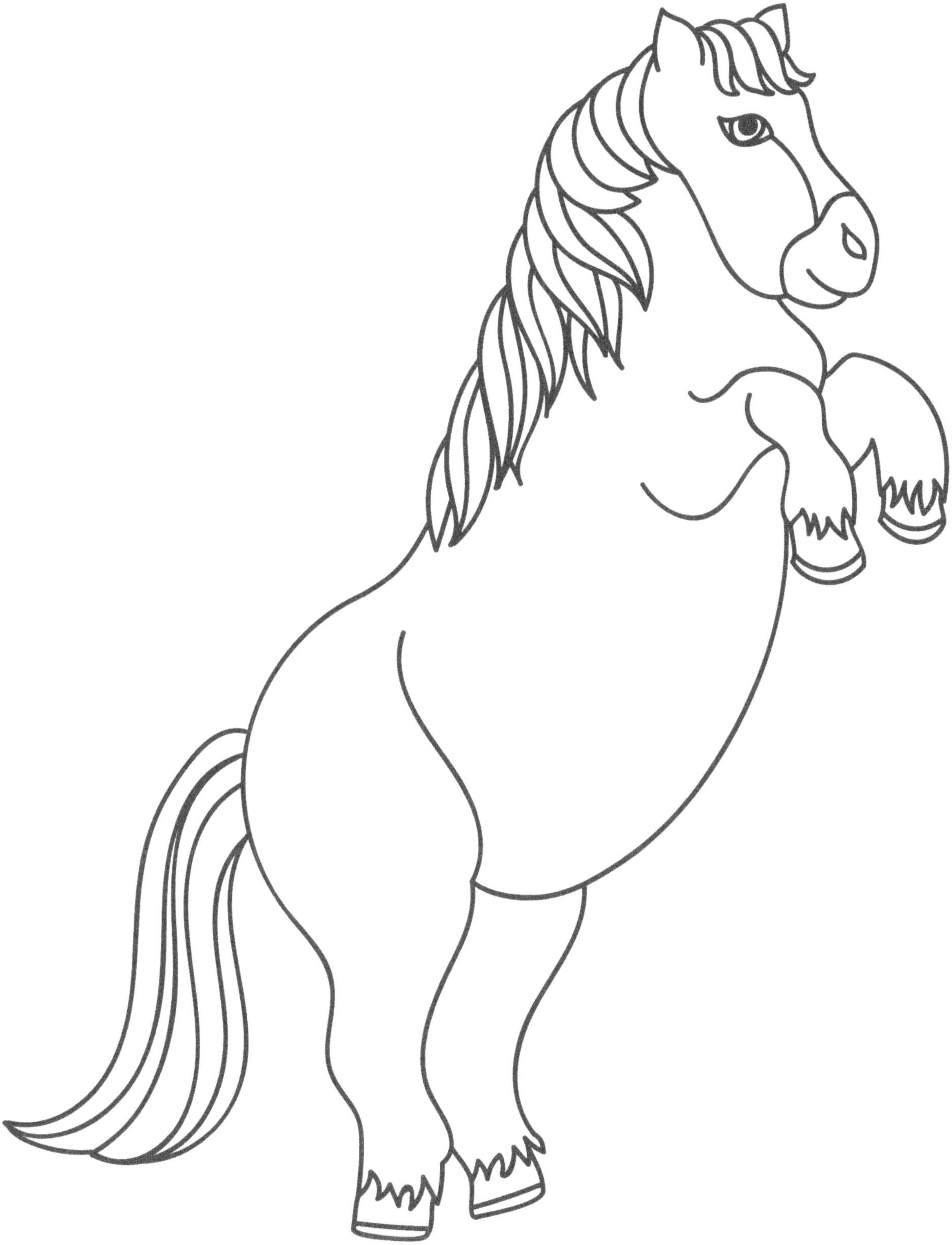

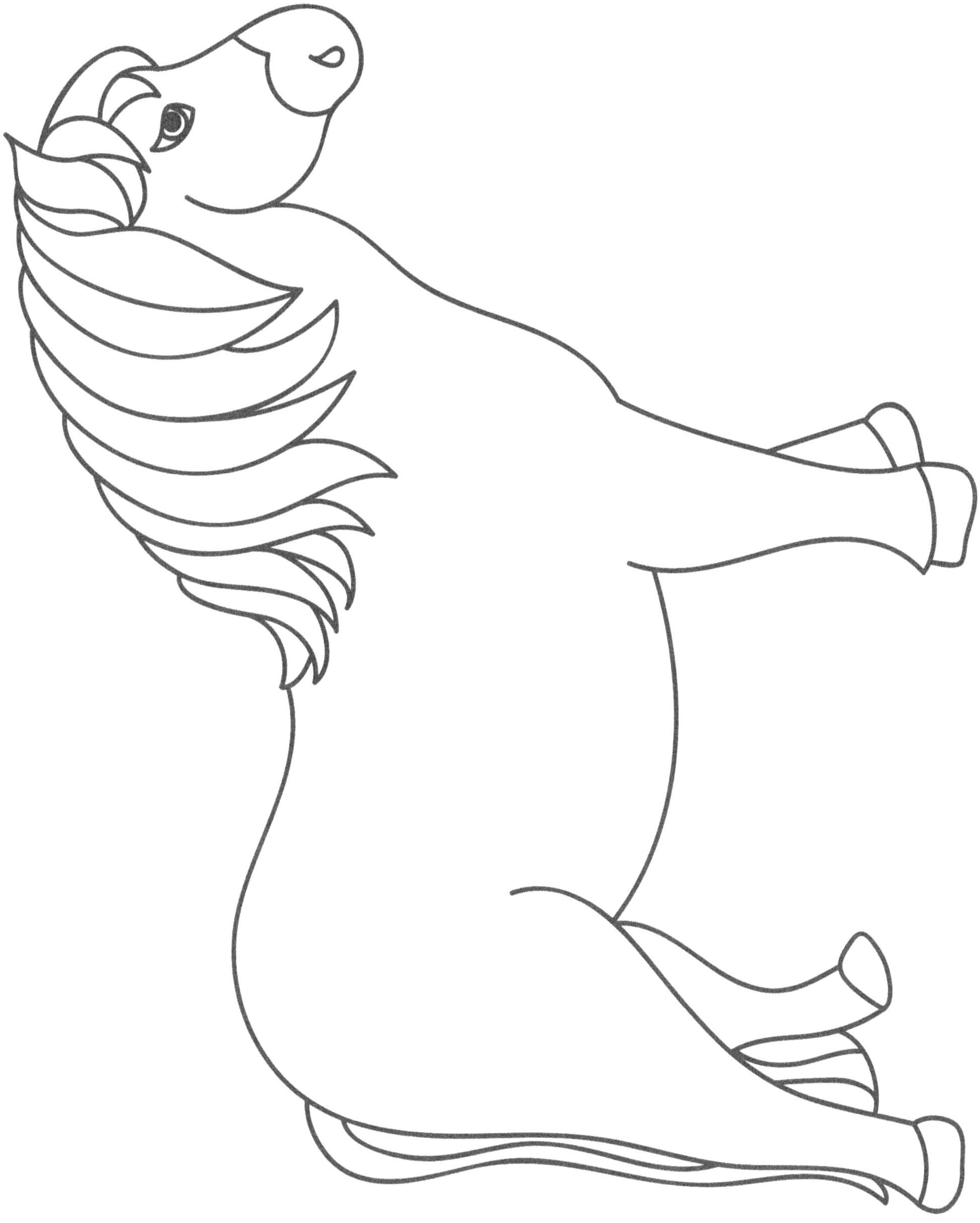

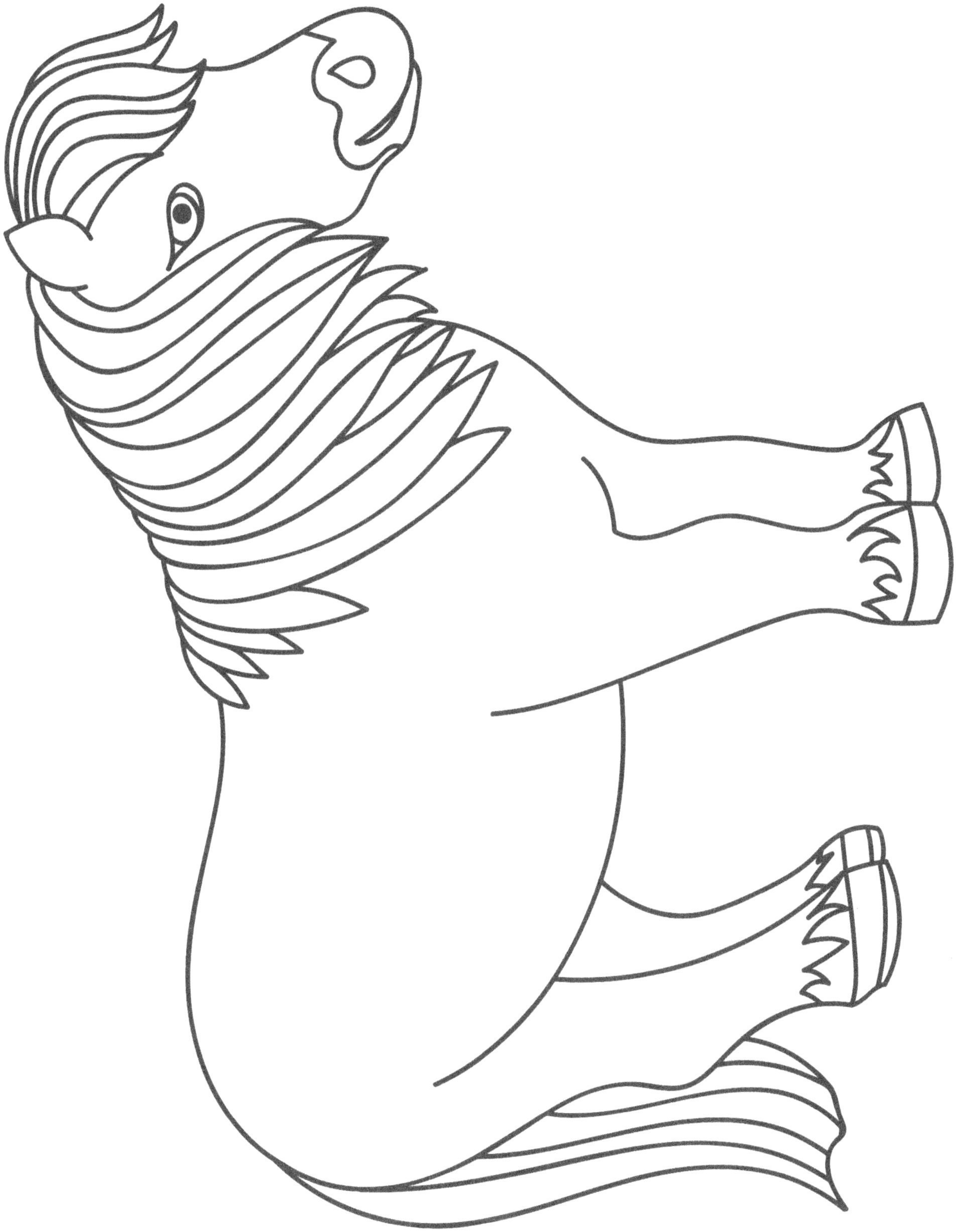

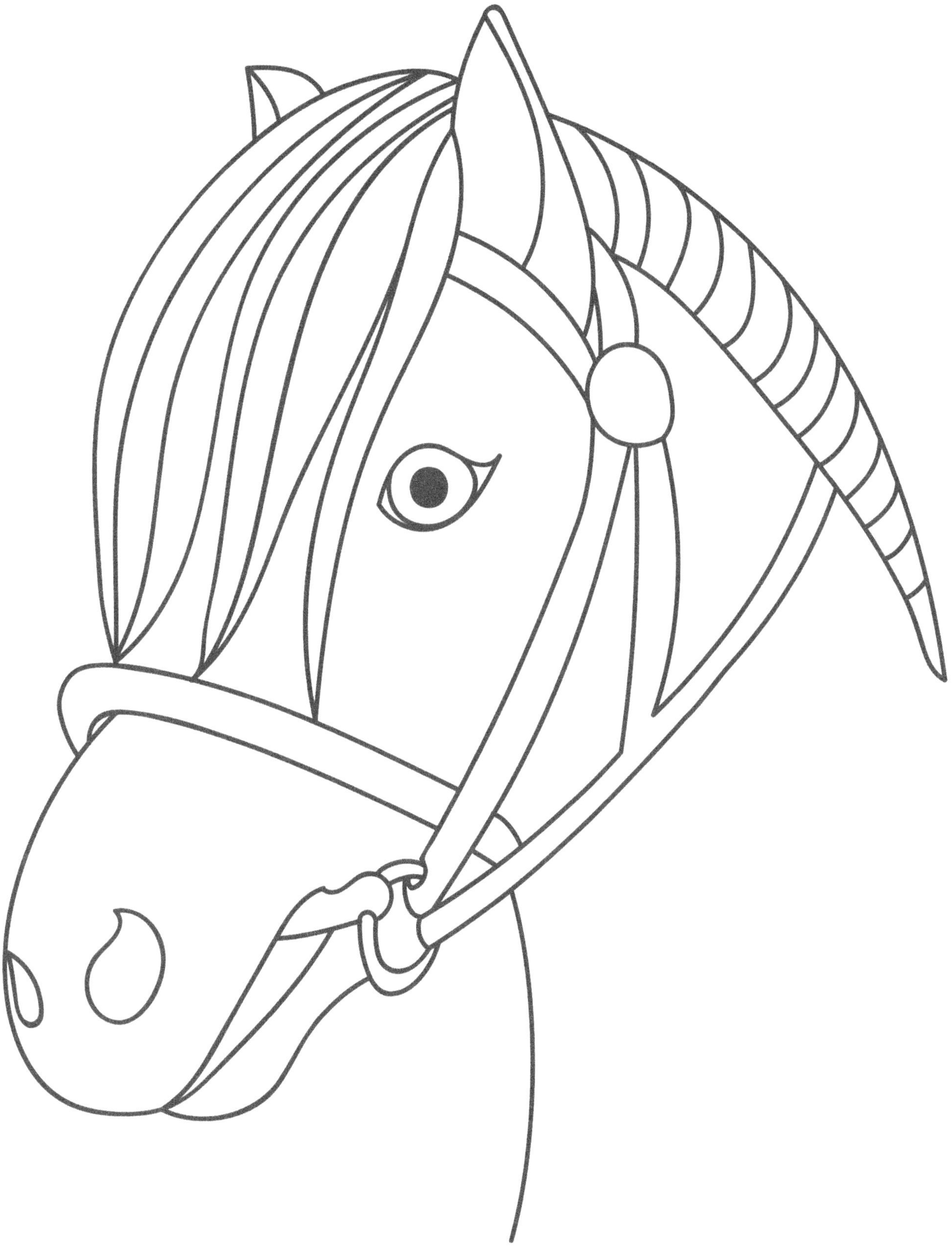

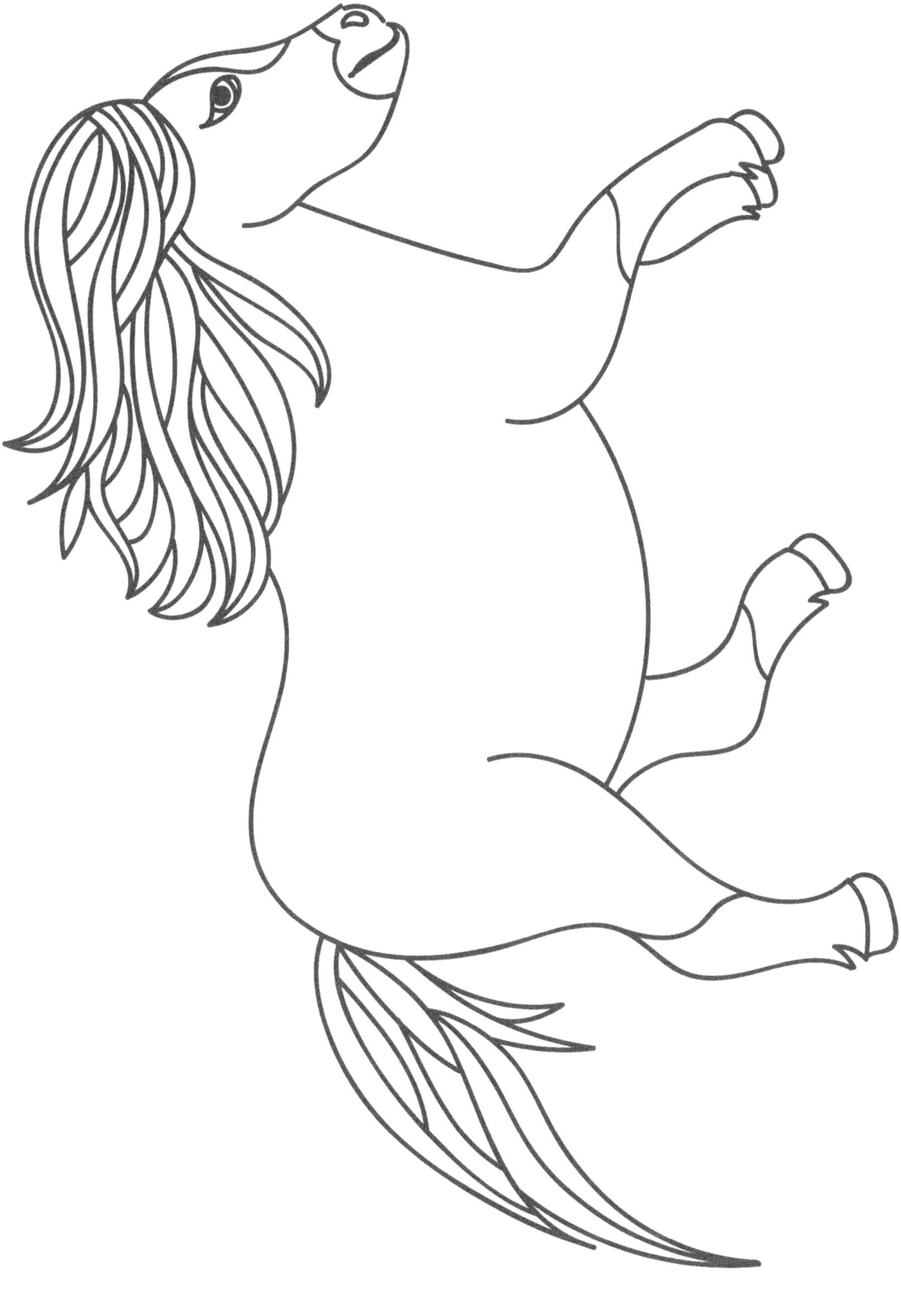

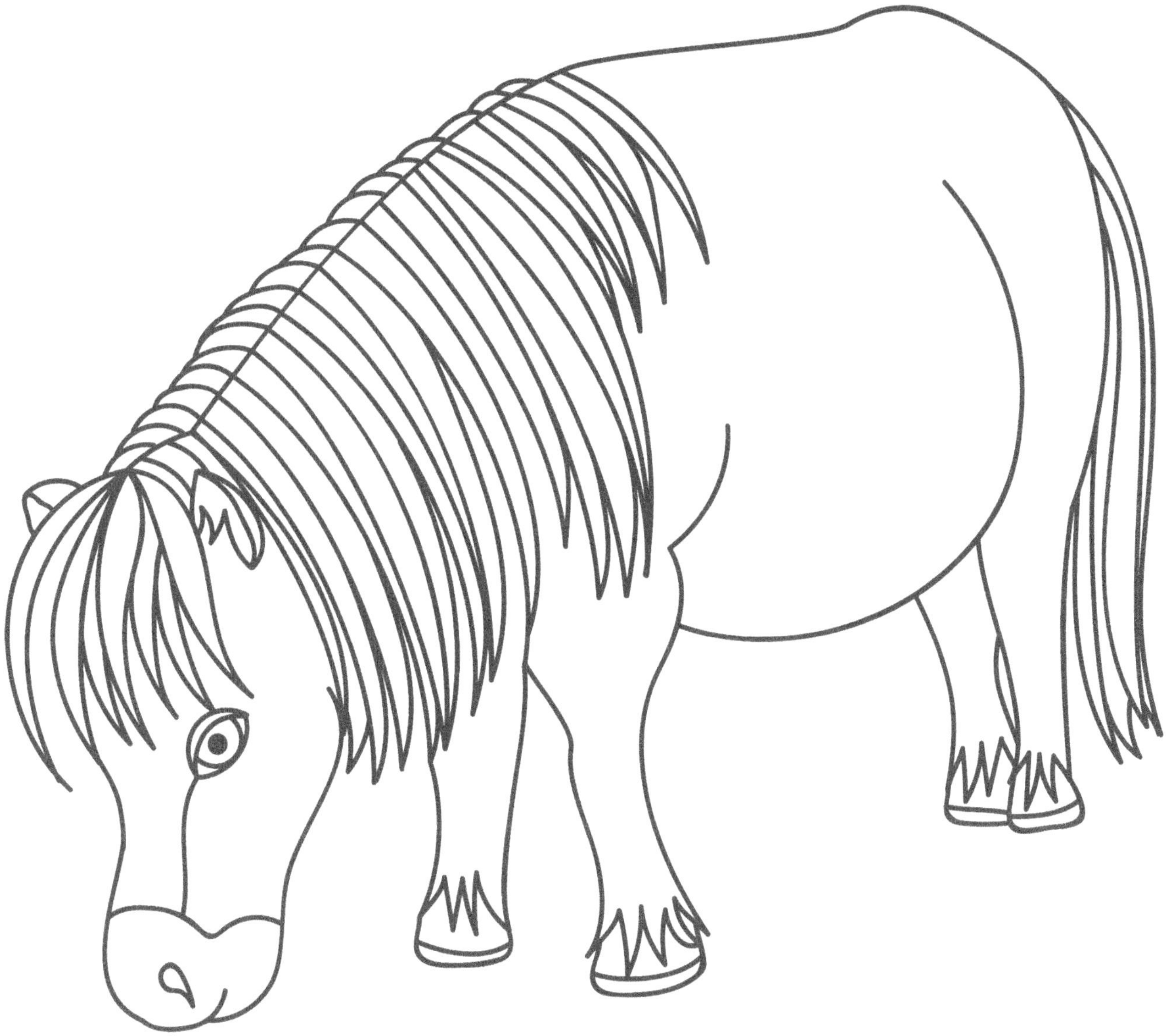

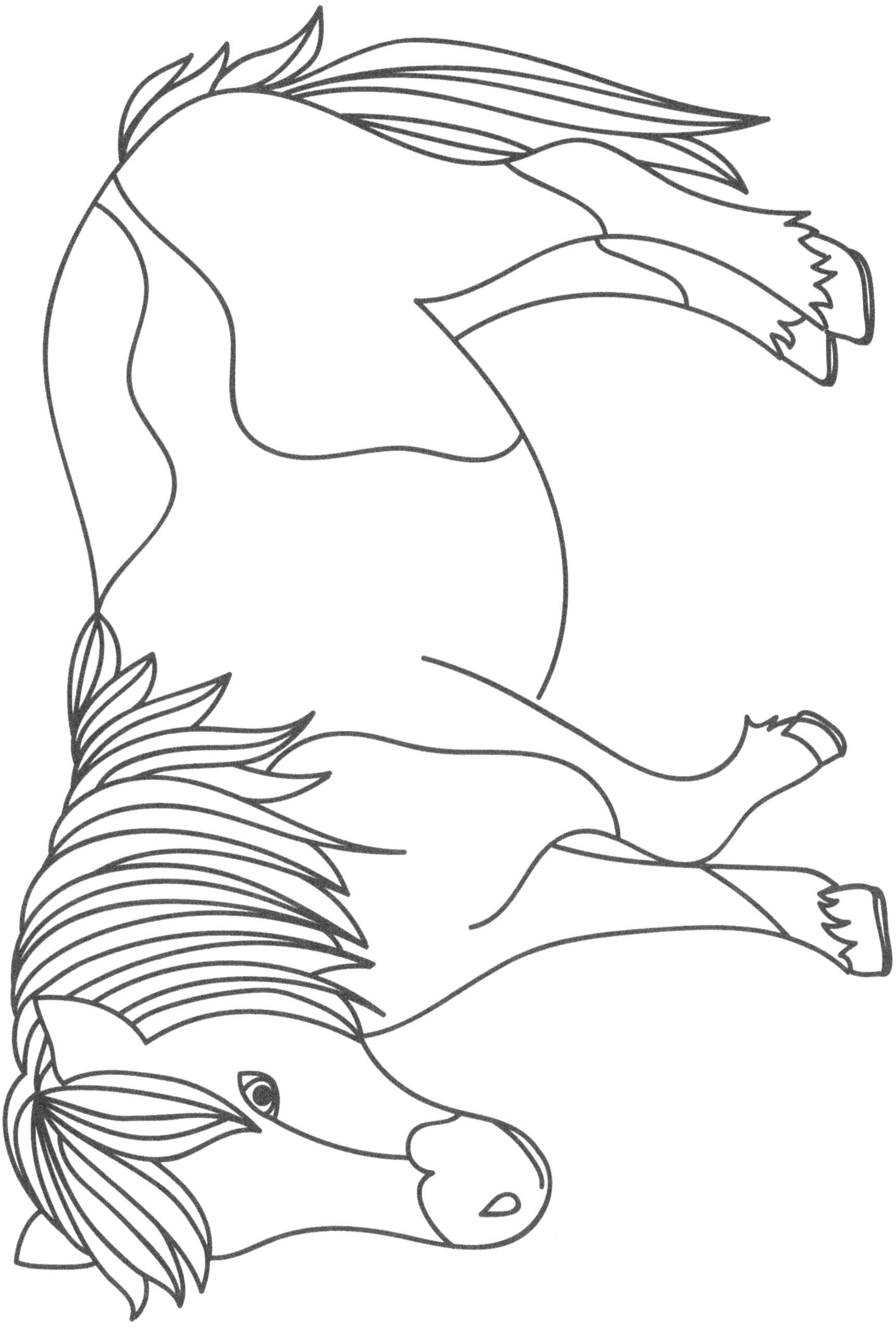

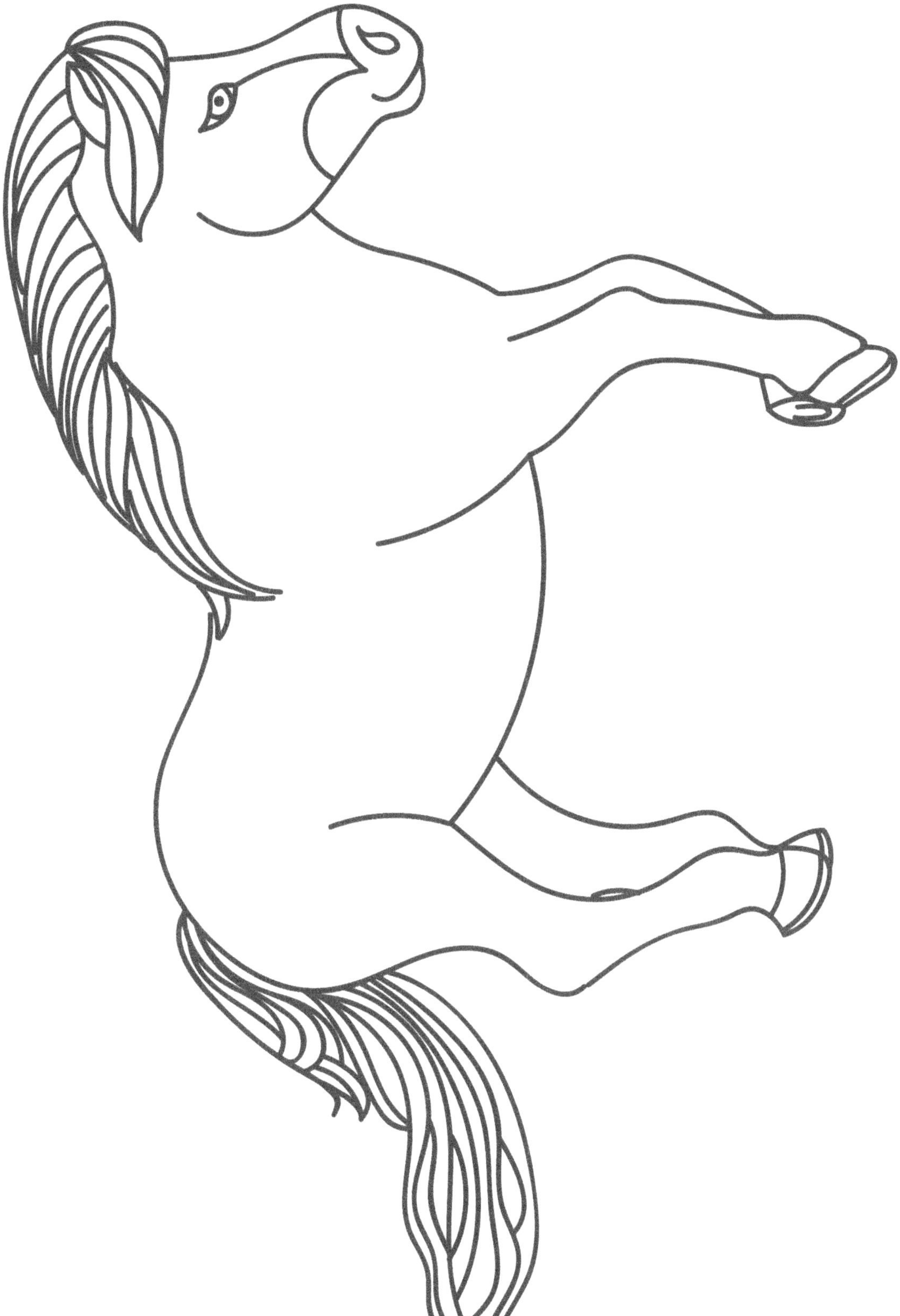

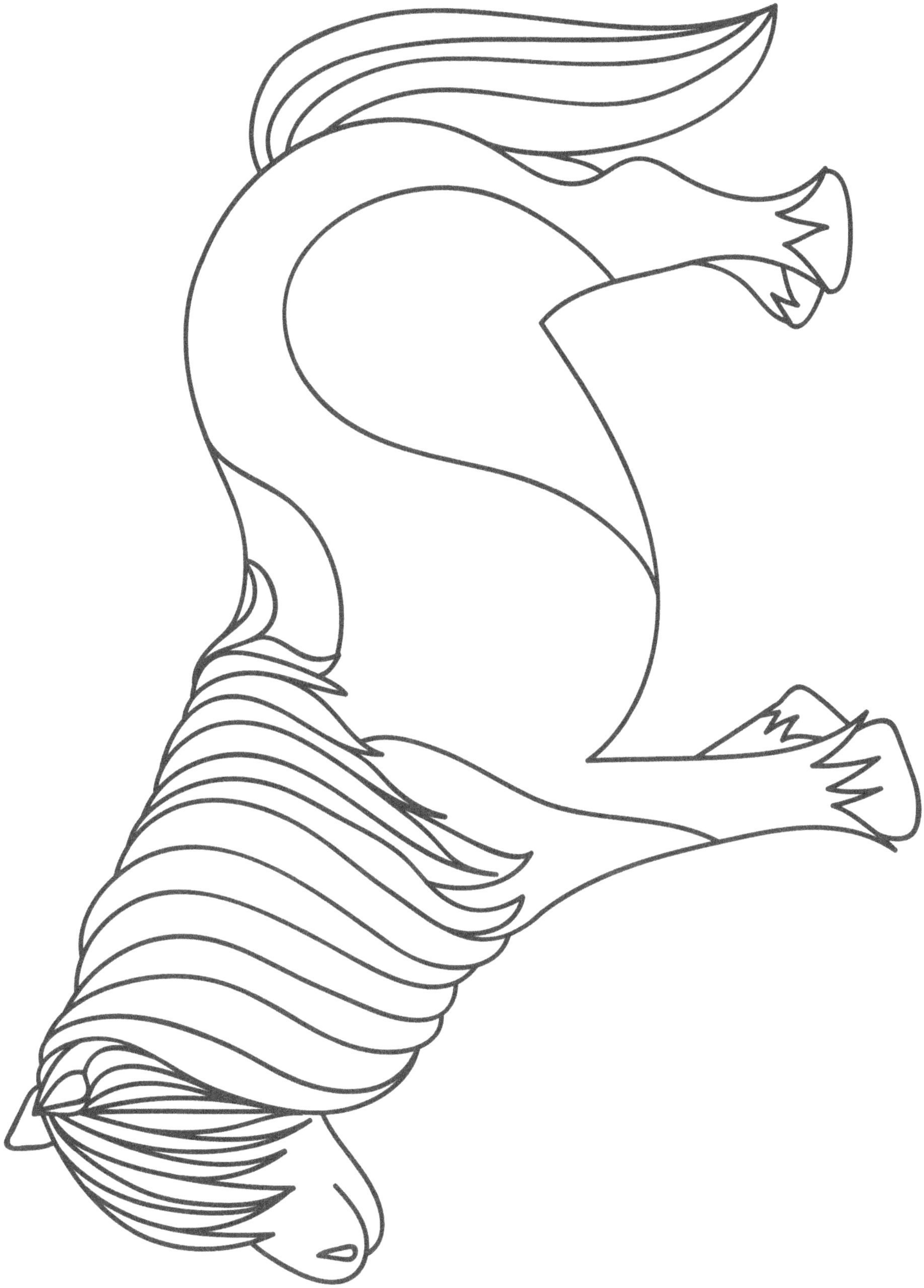

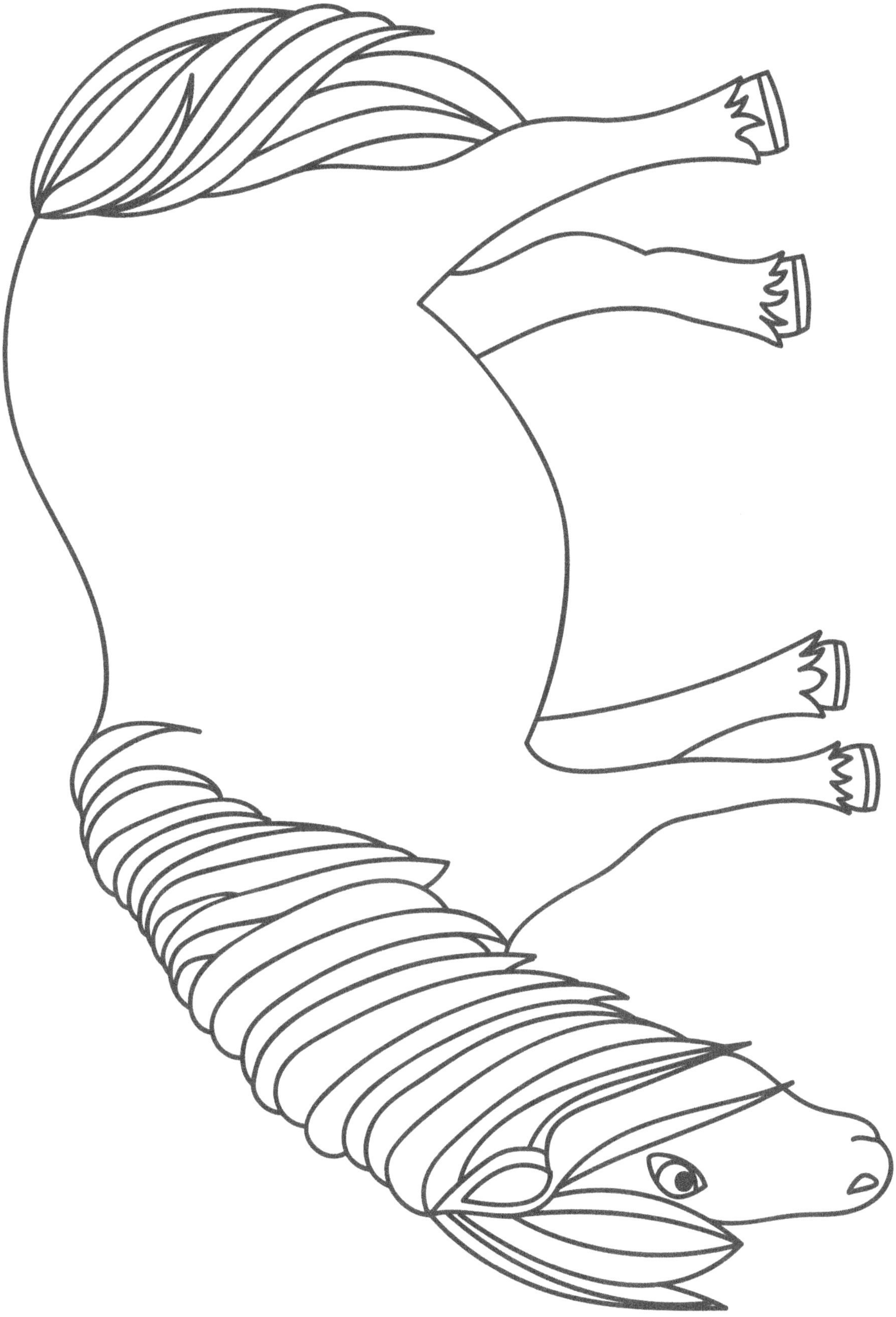

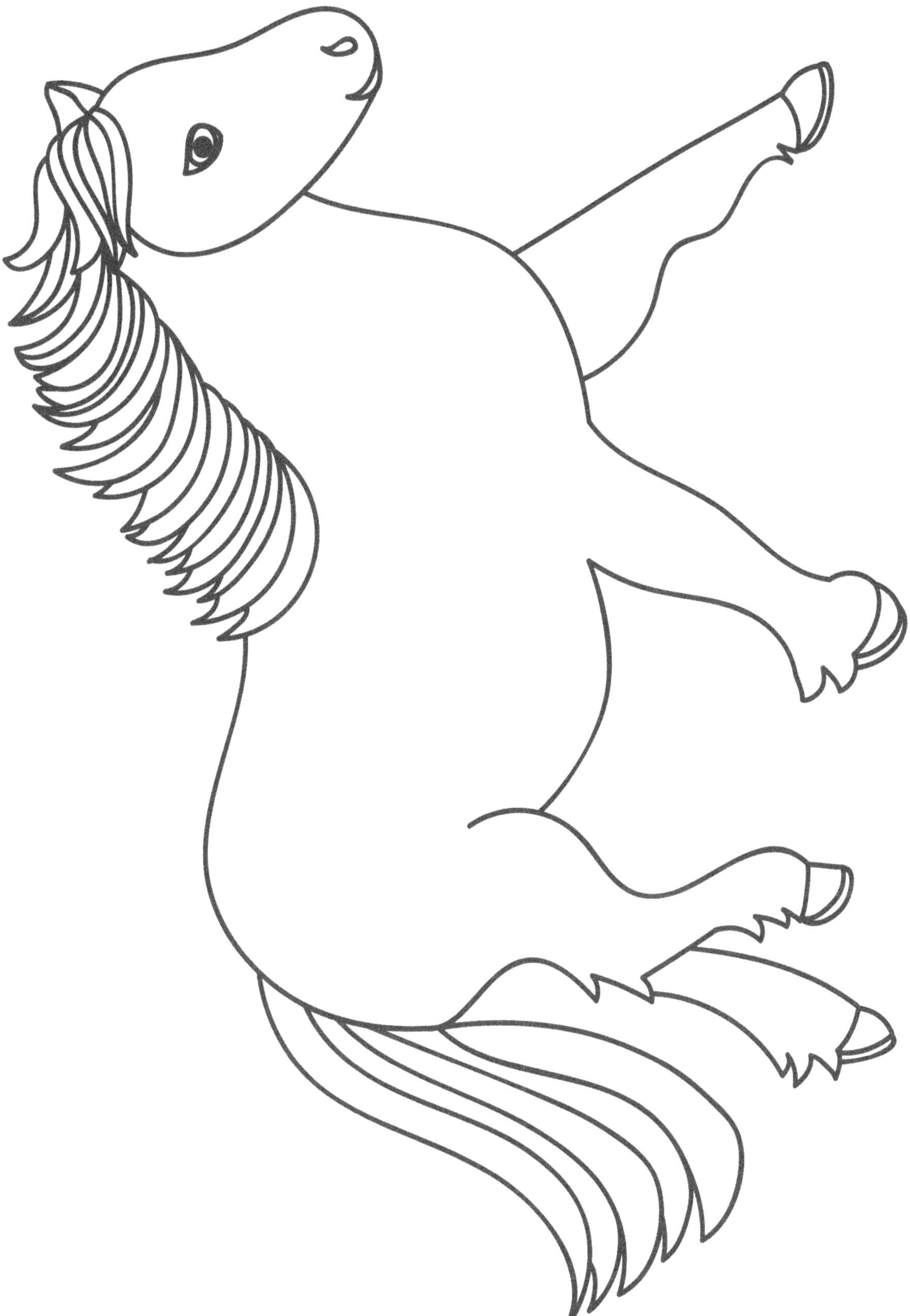

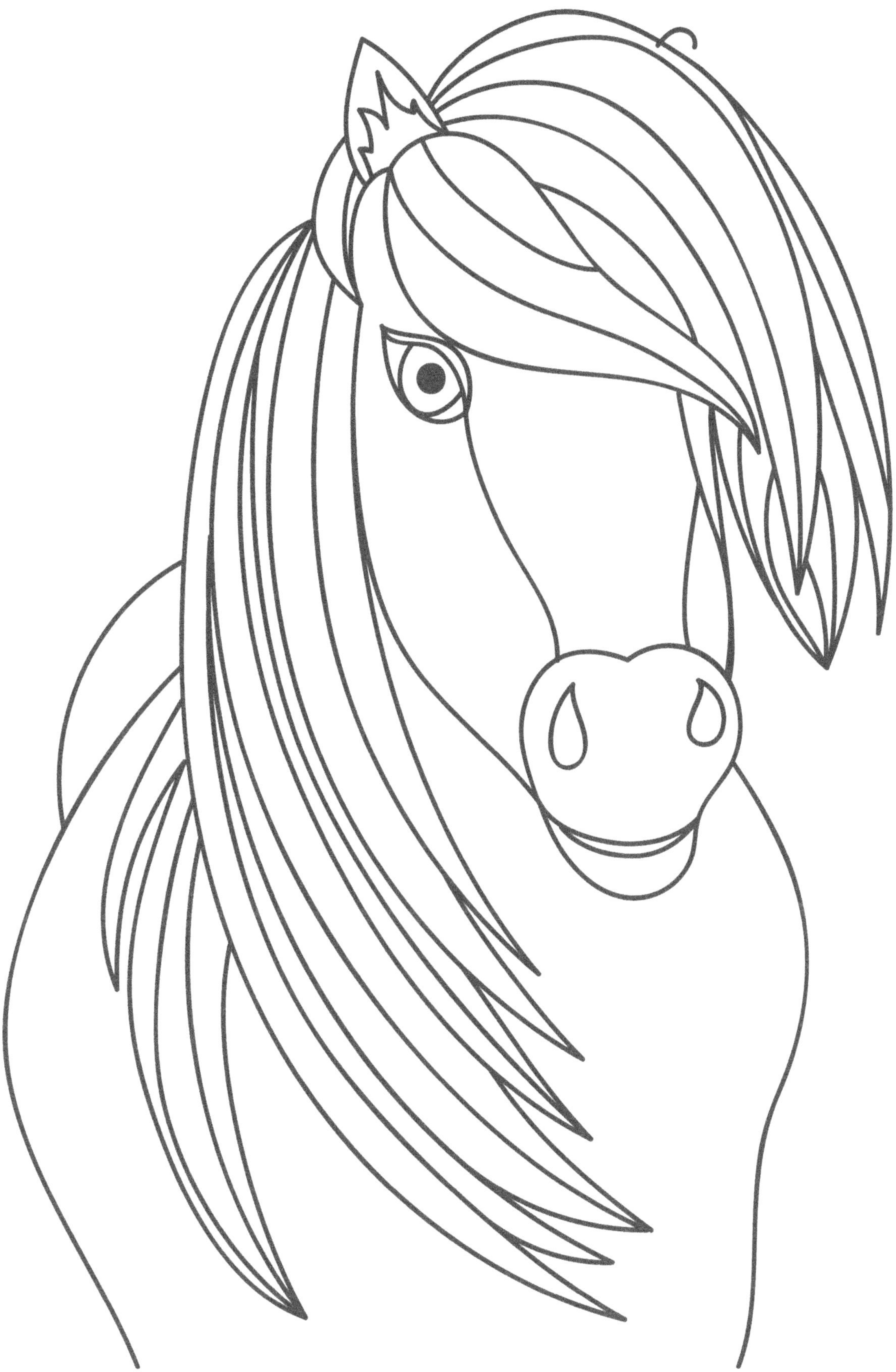

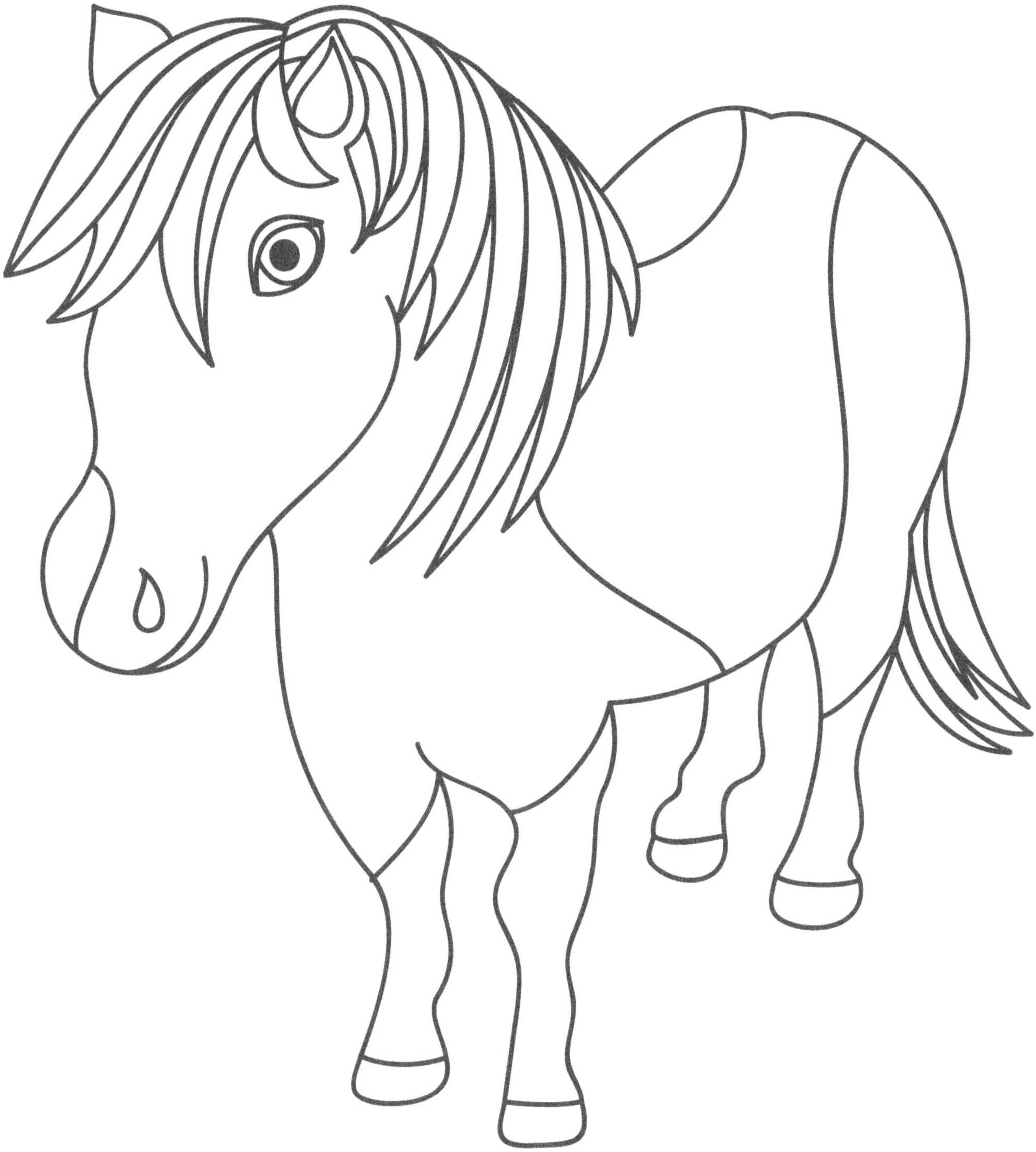

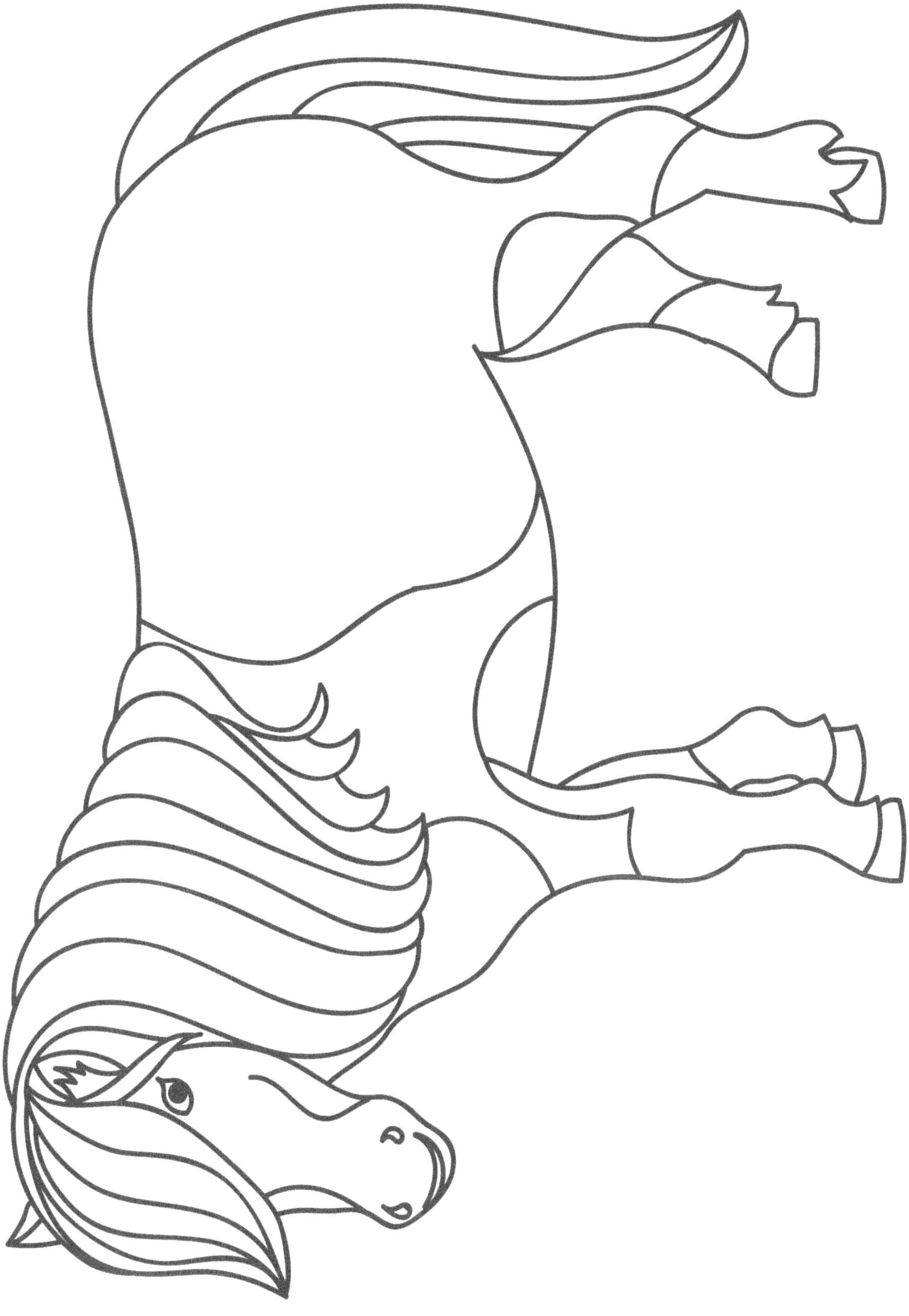

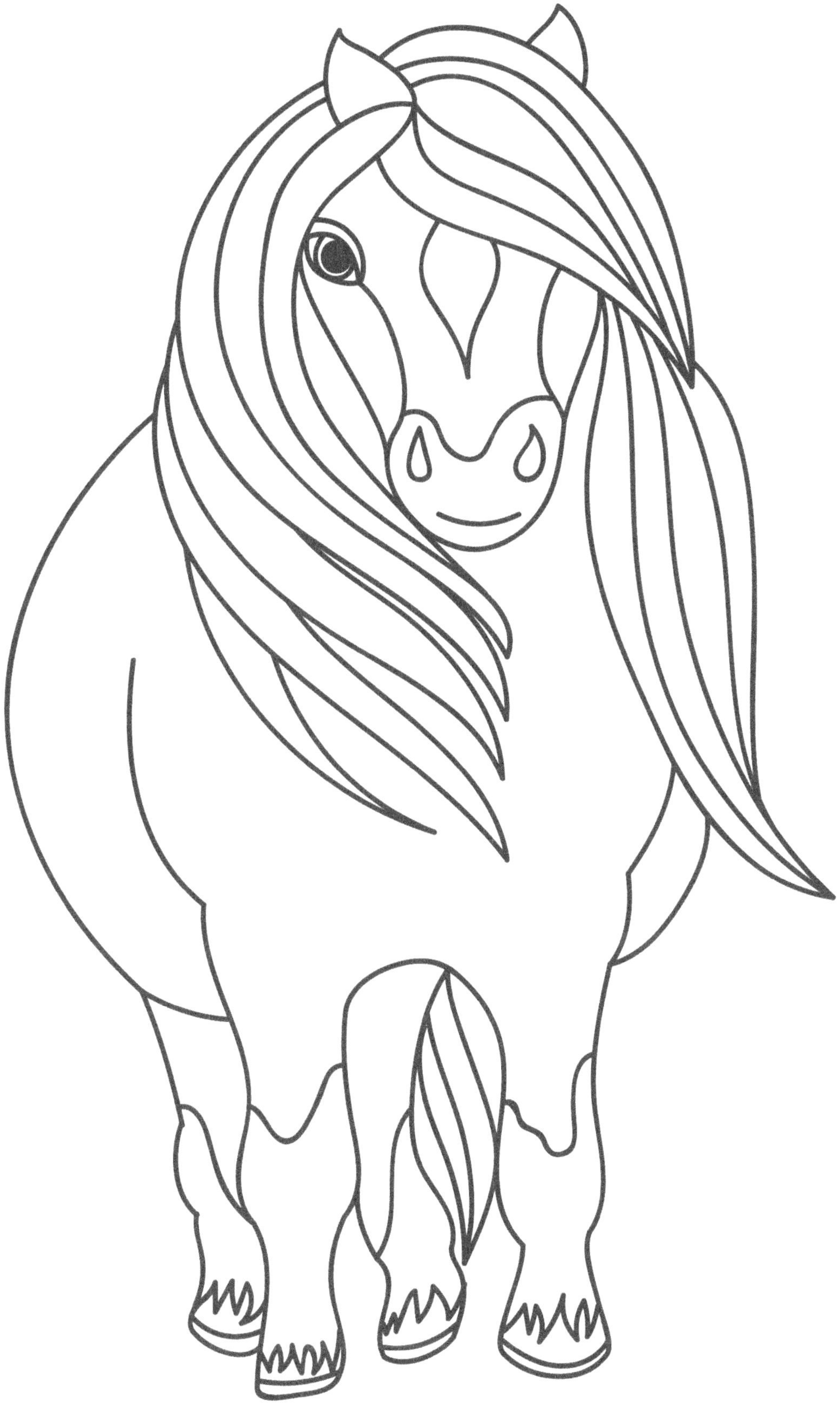

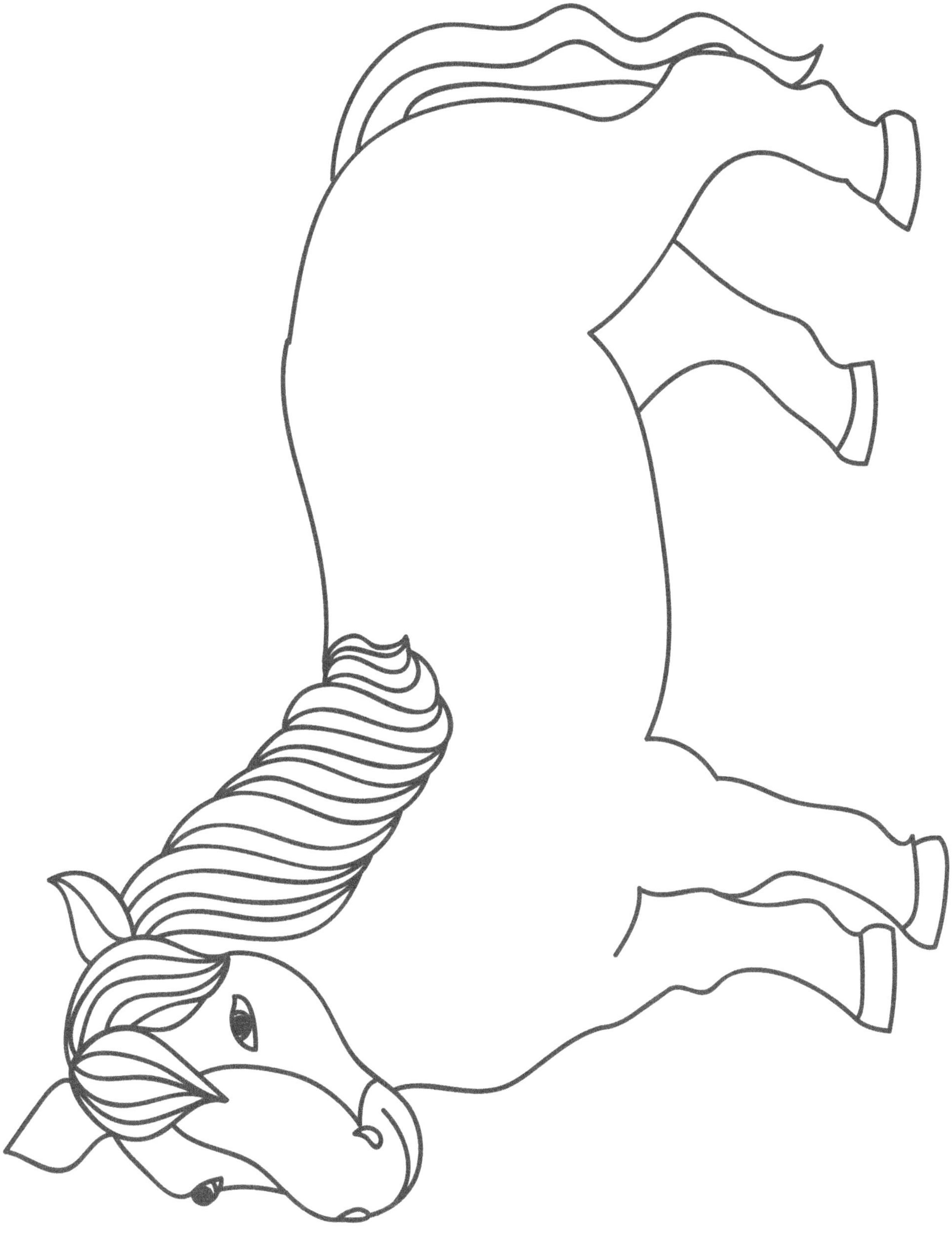

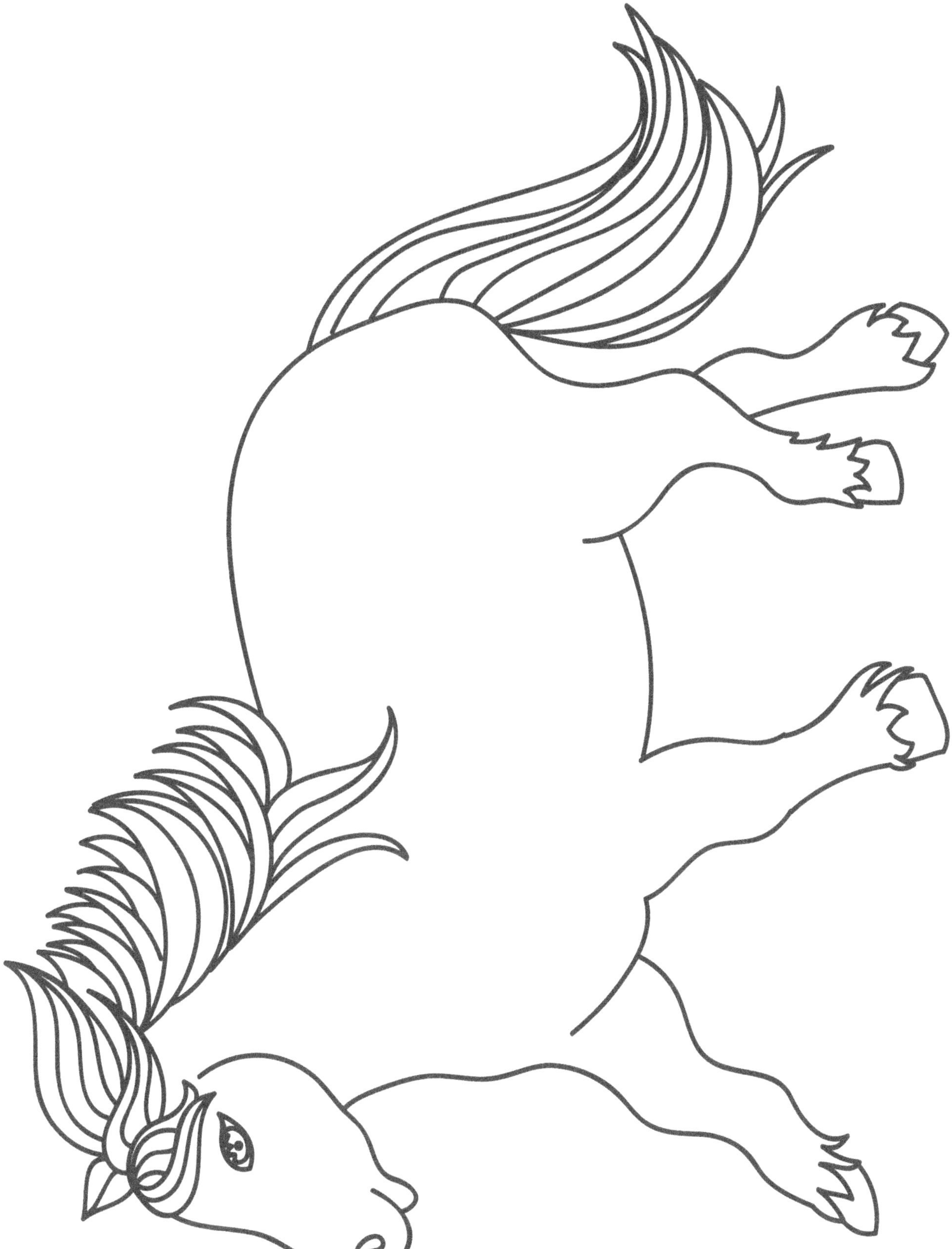

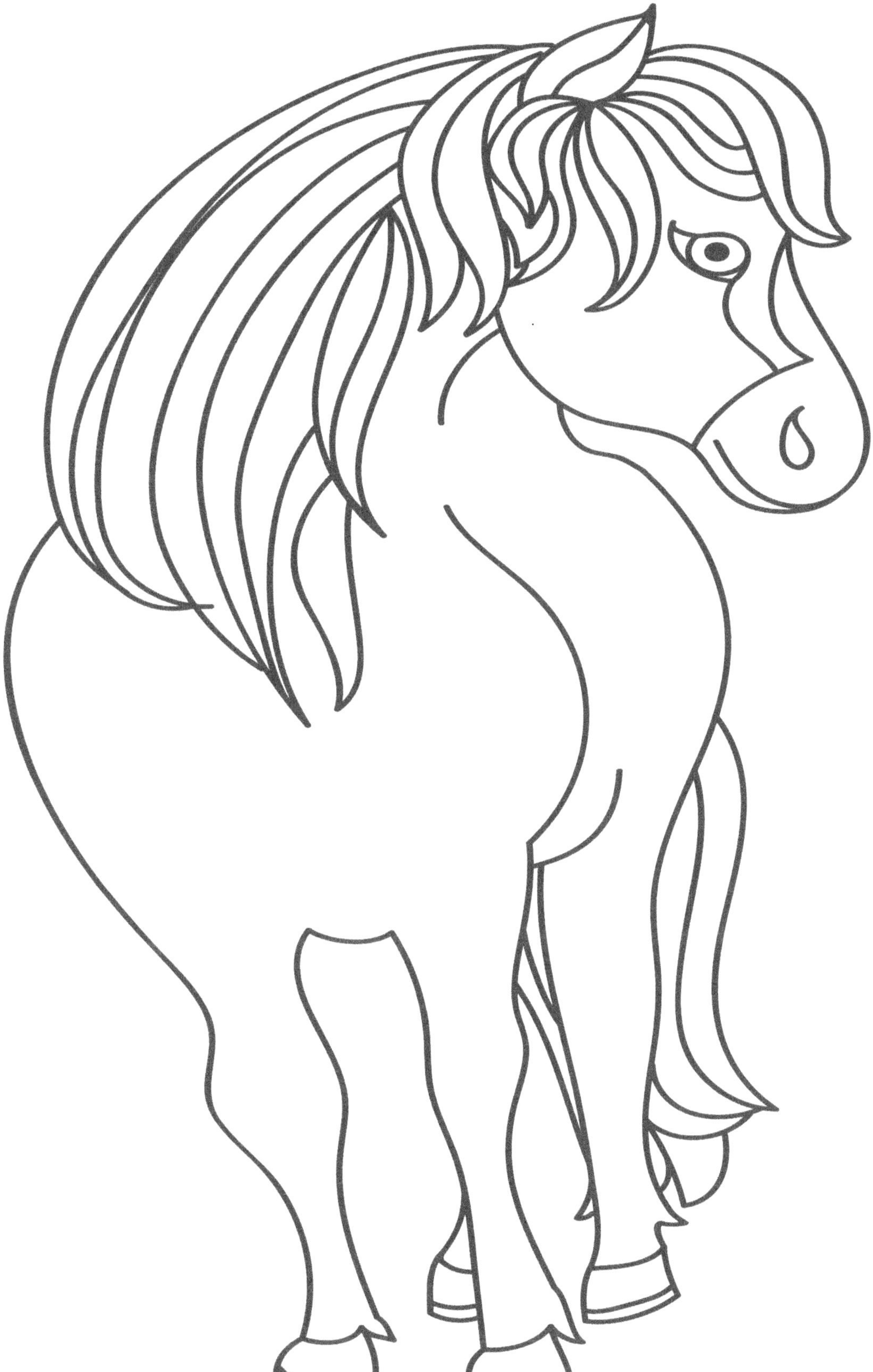

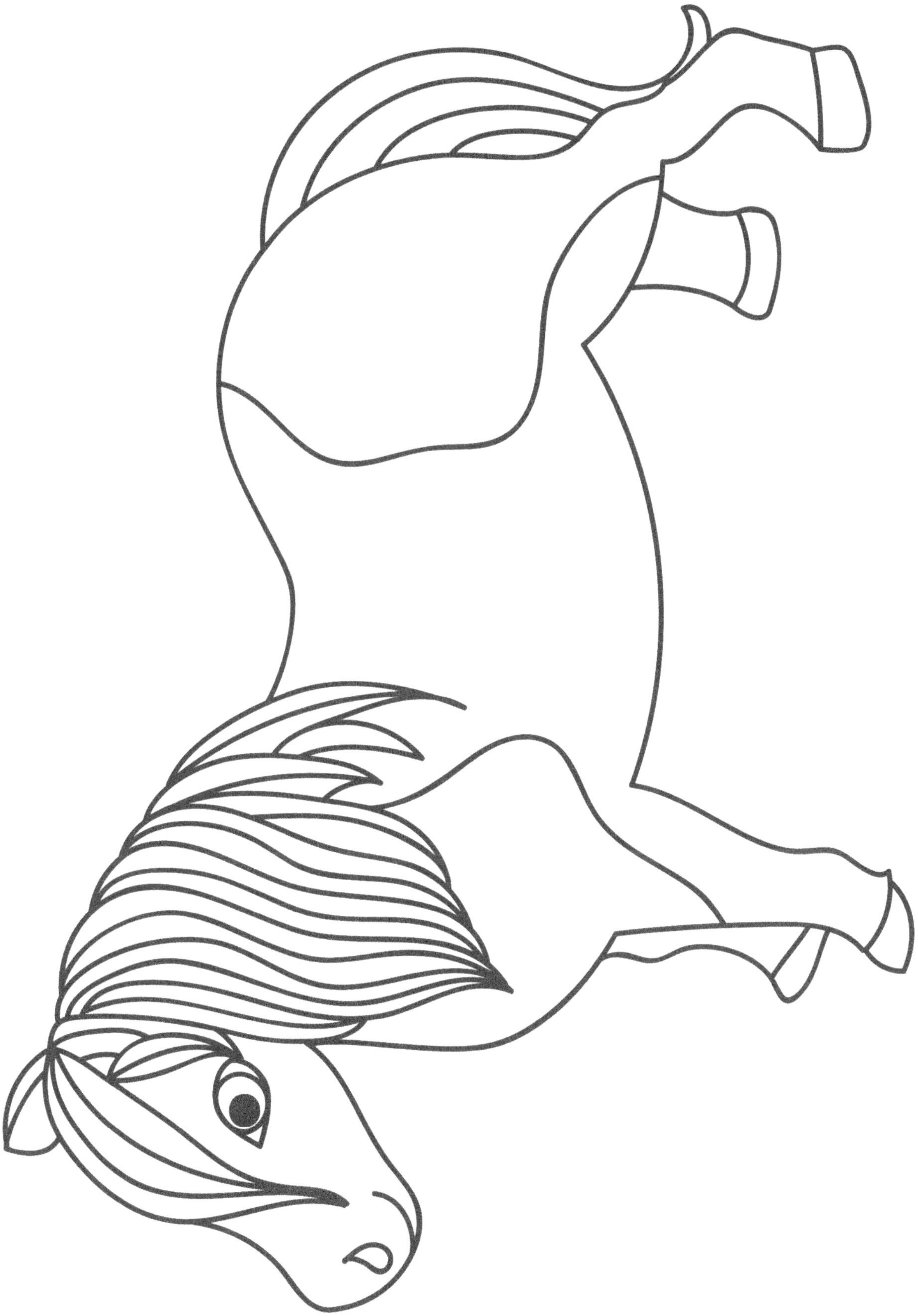

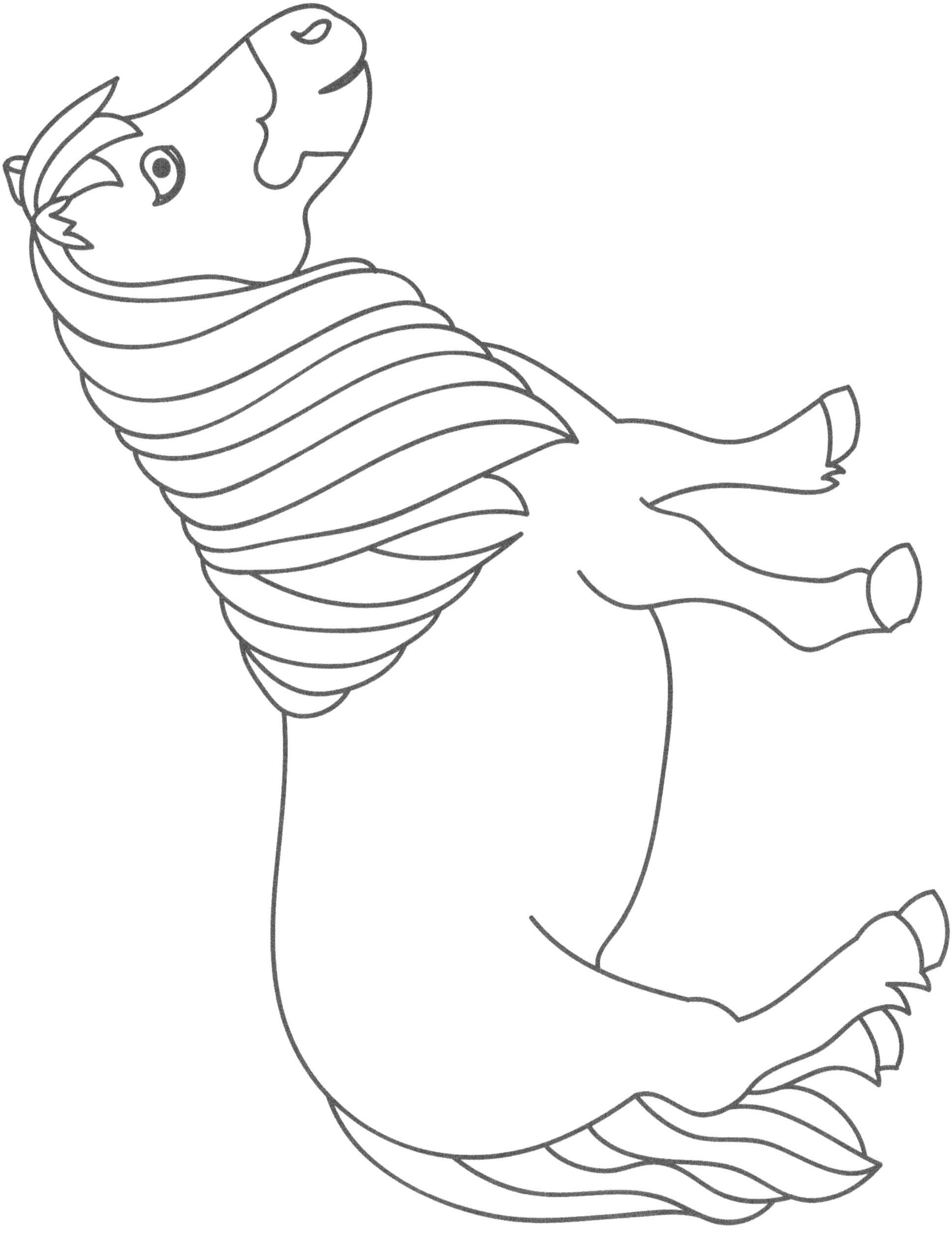

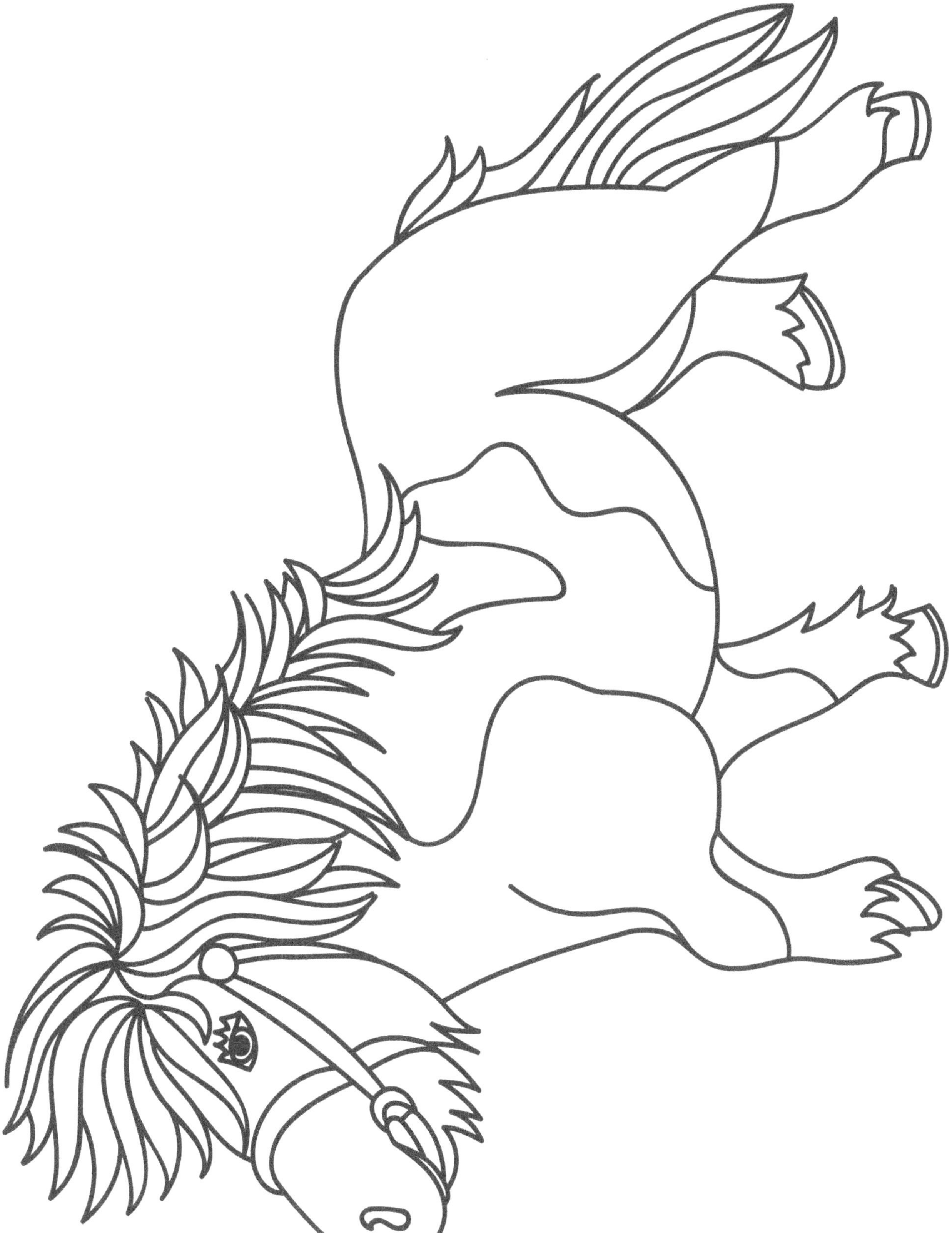

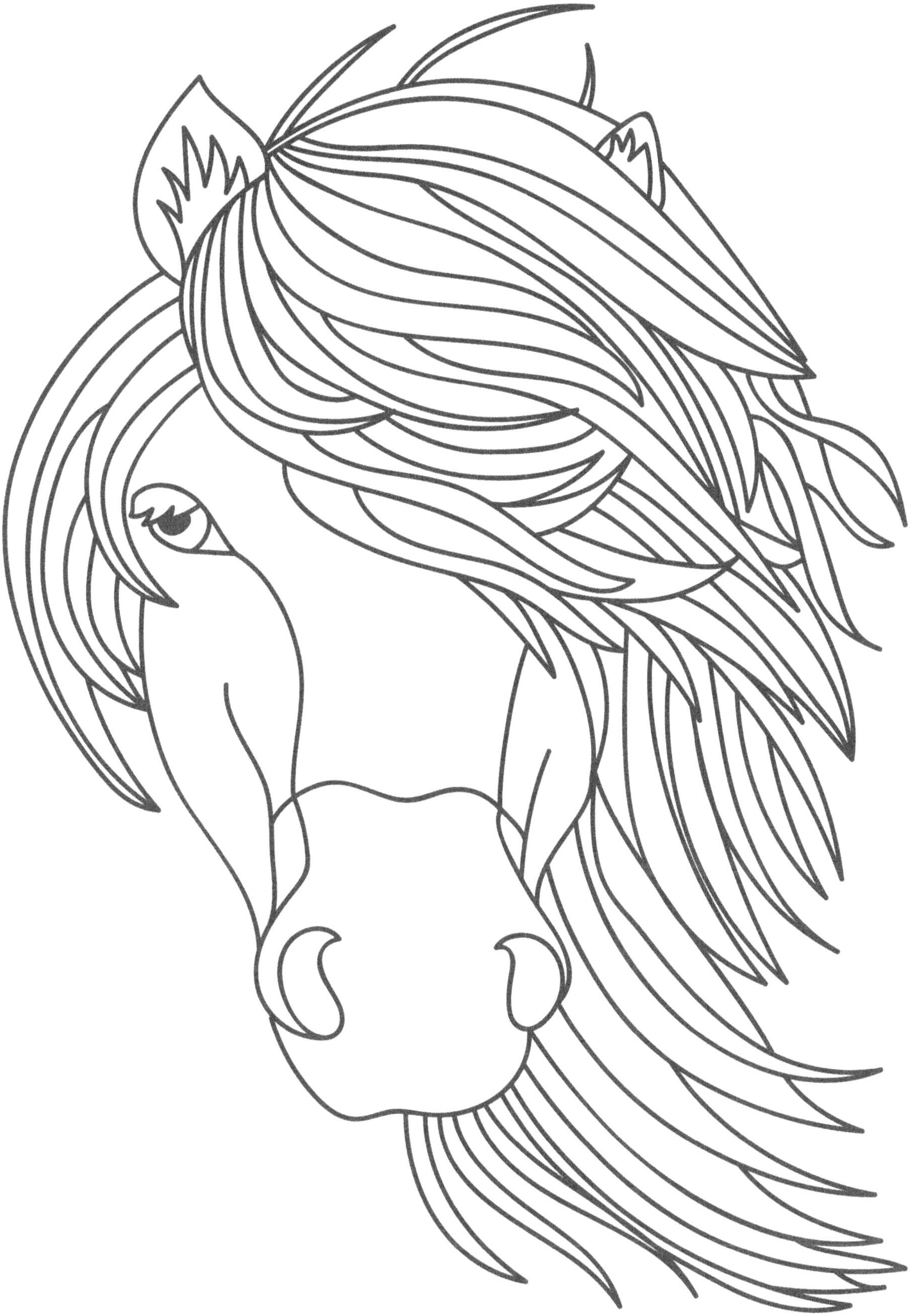

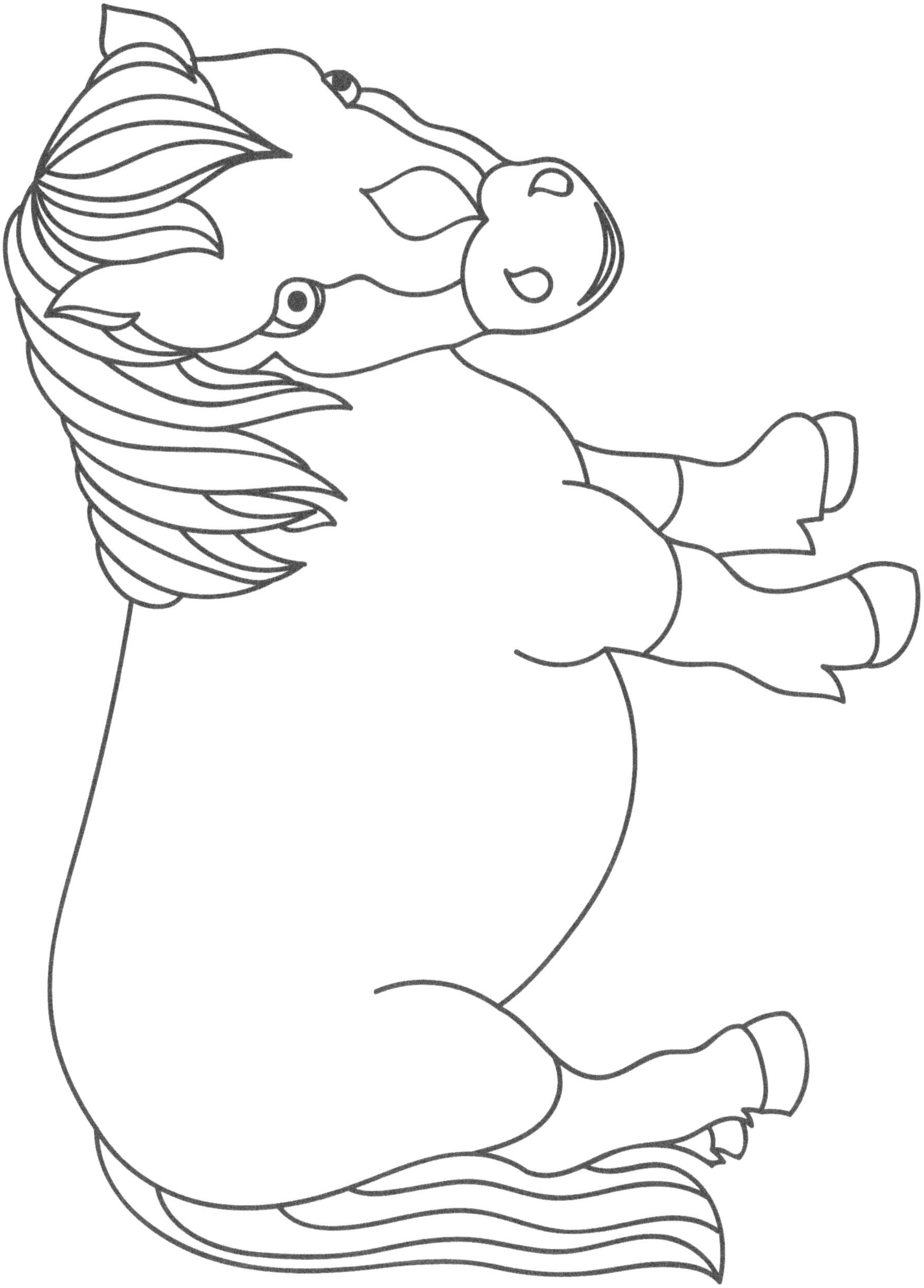

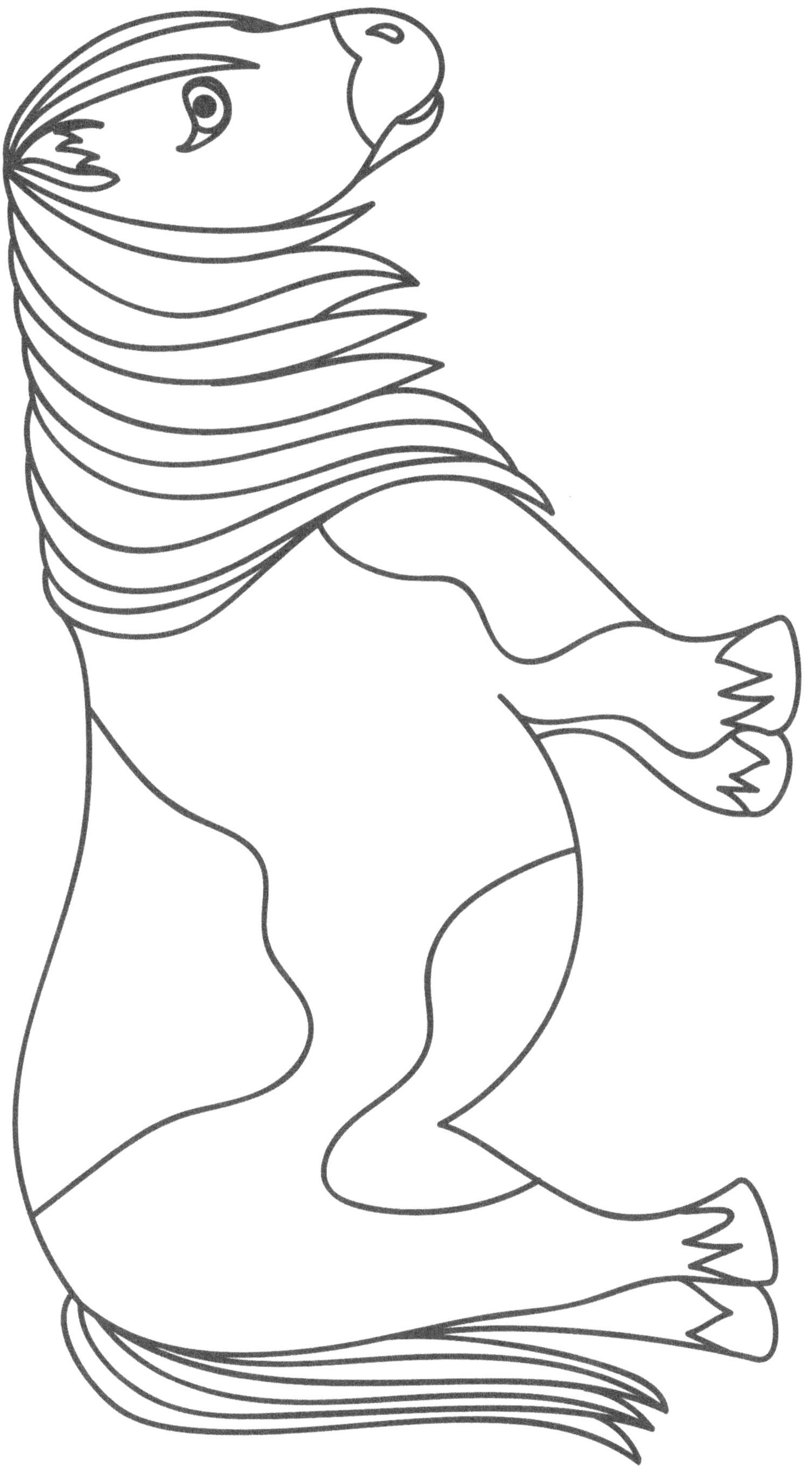

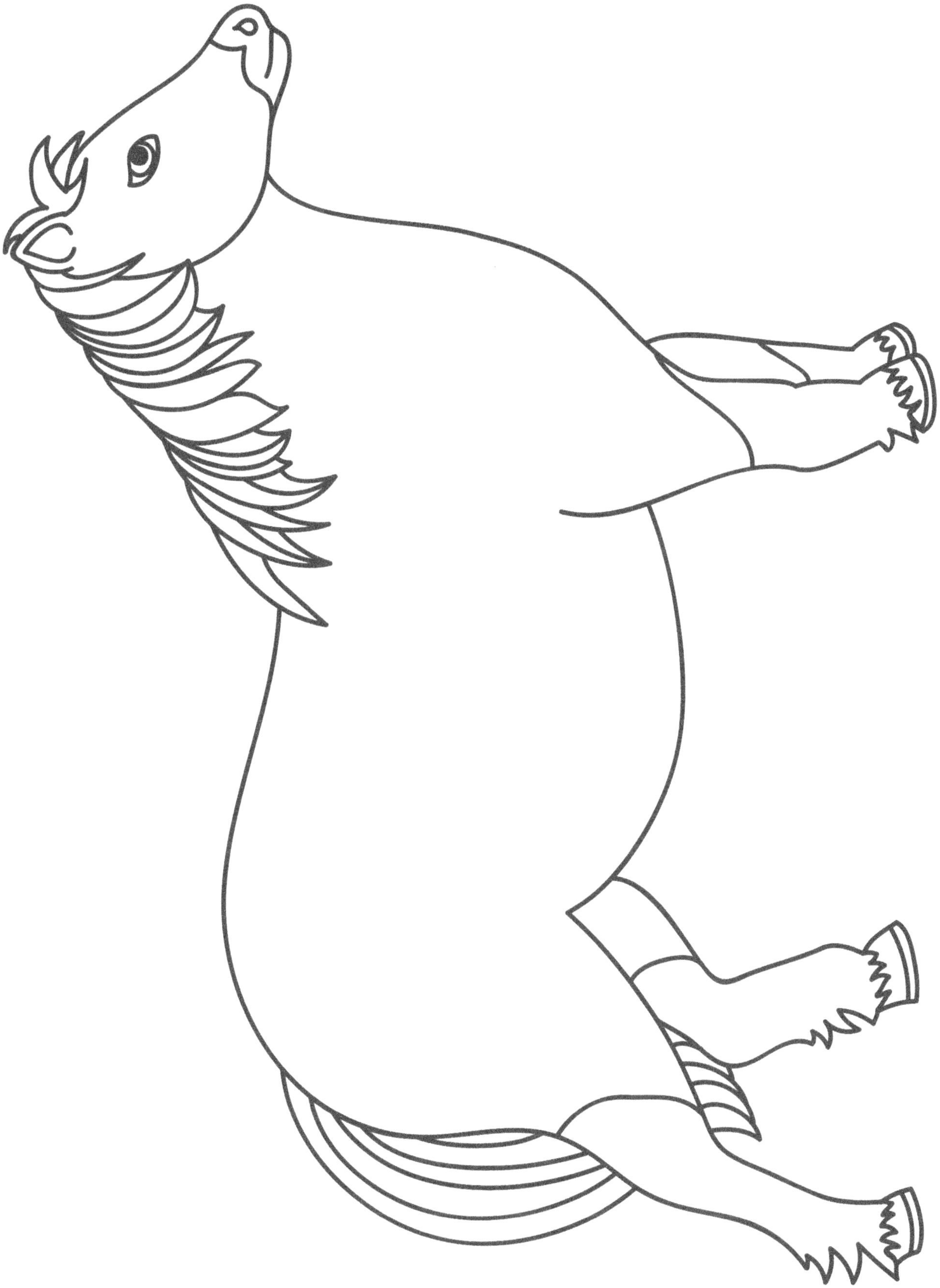

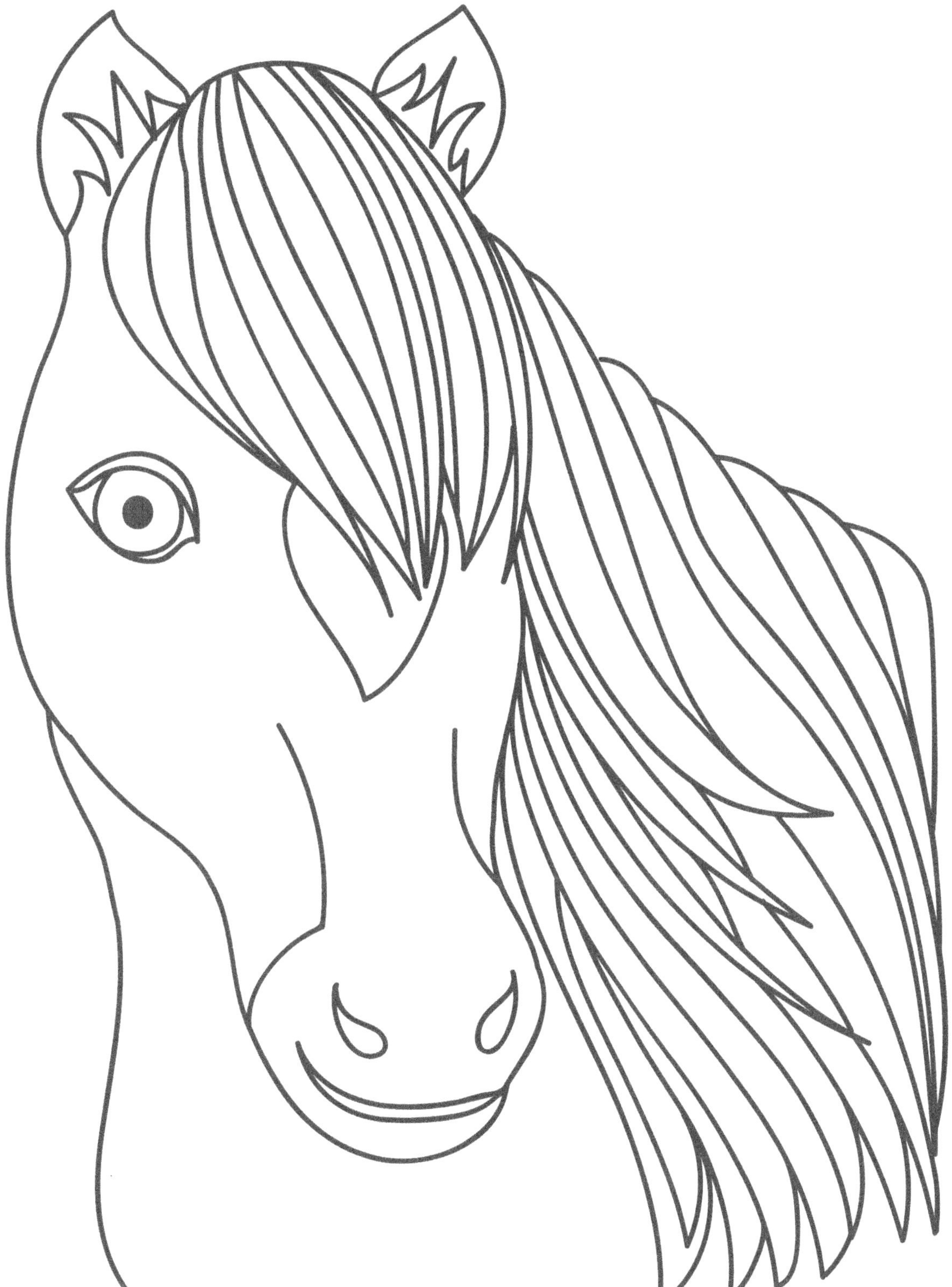

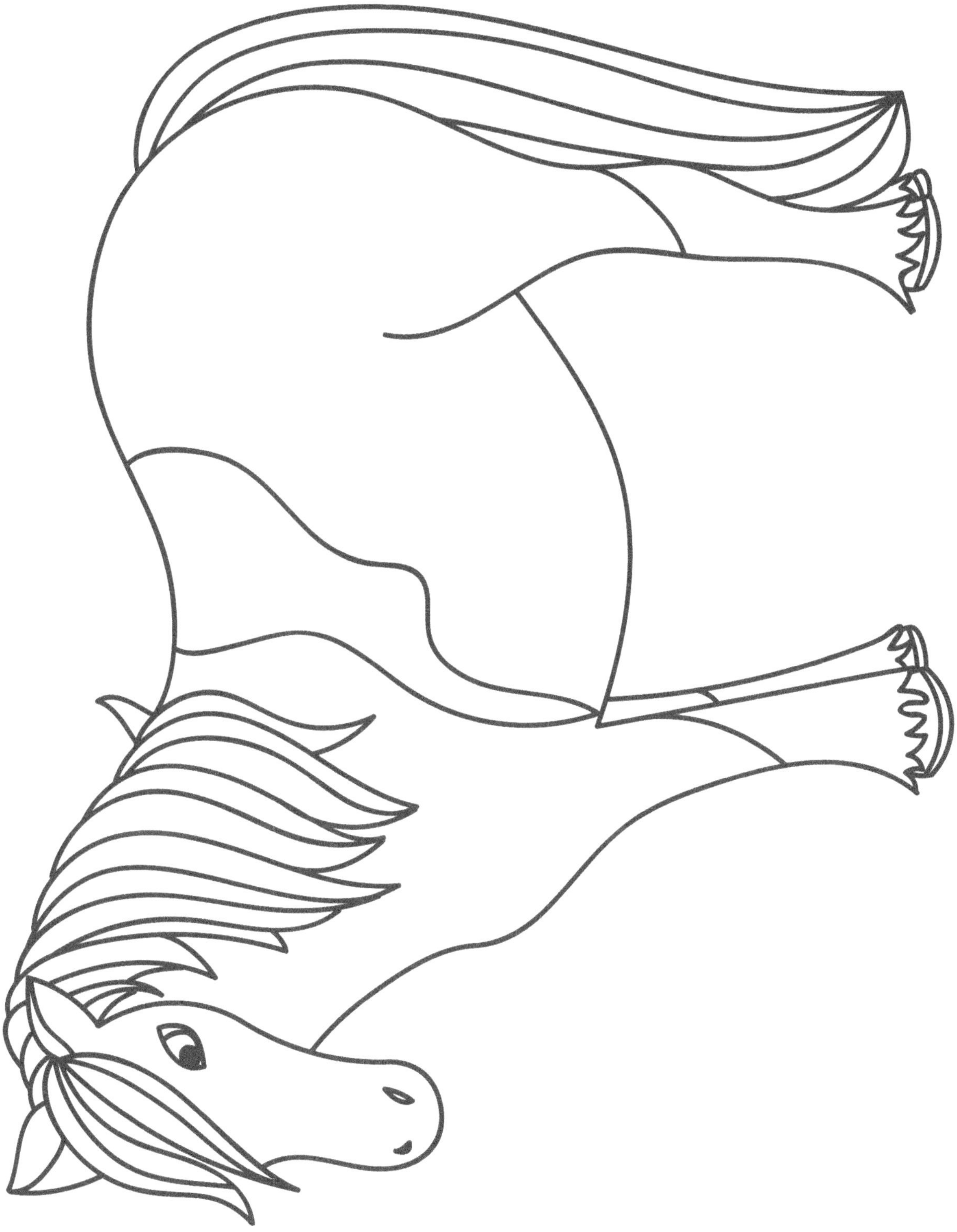

COLOR TEST PAGE

COLOR TEST PAGE